MW01223574

Christian Spoken Word Poems

BRENDA MILLER MEYERS

CHRISTIAN SPOKEN WORD POEMS

iUniverse books may be ordered through booksellers or by contacting:

iUniverse
1663 Liberty Drive
Bloomington, IN 47403
www.iuniverse.com
844-349-9409

ISBN: 978-1-6632-3641-8 (sc)
ISBN: 978-1-6632-3642-5 (e)

Library of Congress Control Number: 2022903481

Print information available on the last page.

iUniverse rev. date: 02/24/2022

Contents

Acknowledgement

I am a member of Northwest Foursquare
Church in Federal Way, WA.

I want to thank all of the pastors and members.

I would also like to give special thanks to
several members of our church:

Anne Kinkade, Celeste and John Riedel for all of their
support when I started writing all of my poems. If they
had not supported me as much as they did I may
have stopped writing after writing my first poem.

Last but not least: I would also like to thank my
Sister/Friend Carolyn Nixon-Coleman for her
continued persistence sharing with me that I
should start back attending church again.

All of you have been a blessing to me! I thank all of you!

Pray

I don't know what to do
I don't know what to say
I do know that I need to Pray
Because I want to be happy today and always!

Now I know what to do
Now I know what to say
I need to Pray
So that I can be happy today and always!

Thank you Lord for your Kindness
It was not you that was my problem it was my Blindness
You have always been there for me this I know is true
And I am always going to put my faith in you!

When doctors were prescribing me drugs
Because of you I was able to put them under my rugs
When I was having hard times
Because of you I never did any crimes
When men were telling me what to do
Because Of you I was able to say that is not true!

Lord it took me a long time to realize that
you have always been there for me

Lord I will always be there for you and I will
always pray for others and me too!

Brenda Miller Meyers
May 8, 2021

Lord, Because of You

I am so proud
Now I can speak out loud
I am so blessed
Lord because of You!

Lord when I kept thinking that my life was a Mess
Now I know that you were just putting me through a Test
Because of you now my life has been Blessed!
Lord, Because of You!

When I was going through Stress
I keep making my Life a Mess
Lord because of you I am no longer
Stressed I am truly Blessed!

I am so proud I can speak out loud
Lord, Because of You!

Brenda Miller Meyers
May 29, 2021

Lord we hear you

Lord please take this Covid away
So many of us are dying everyday

Lord we hear you
We need to Pray

Lord we want to go and visit a family member and a friend
The fear of this Covid is getting under our skins

Lord we hear you
We need to Pray

Yes it is also called the Pandemic
I know none of us want to be in it

Lord we hear you
We need to Pray

Every since this Pandemic hit
People are losing jobs and some have quit

People are losing homes and some can't pay rent

Crimes have increased
And more people are living on the streets

Blessed our Doctors, Nurses and First Responders
If it wasn't for them more people may have gone under

Lord we hear you
We need to Pray

Because of this Covid/Pandemic

There have been so many changes in our Public Schools
Now Teachers, Parents and Students
have concerns about the new rules

We are all praying that this stops today

Yes we hear you Lord
We need to Pray

Brenda Miller Meyers
June 9, 2021

The Dictionary of Lord I know

When I am Angry, Bored, Crude, Doubtful
I know where to go
To my Bible
Why, Lord because you told me so

When I am Empty, Fearful, Grudging, Hateful,
I know where to go
To my Bible
Why, Lord because you told me so

When I am Indifferent, Judgemental, Kindliness, Lonely,
I know where to go
To my Bible
Why, Lord because you told me so

When I am Mean, Nasty, Opinionated, Picky, Questionable,
I know where to go
To my Bible
Why, Lord because you told me so

When I am Rude, Scared, Tired, Unfaithful
I know where to go
To my Bible
Why, Lord because you told me so

When I am Vindictive, Withdrawn, Xanadu, Yelling
I know where to go
To my Bible
Why, Lord because you told me so

When I am Zigzagging,
I know where to go
To my Bible
Why, Lord because you told me so

If you see something on this list that you can relate to
I just want you to know that I can too

Now I am Reading my Bible
Now I am Blessed and Thankful!
And you can too!
Why? Because God tells you so!

Thank You Lord!
Brenda Miller Meyers June 2. 2021

What Christians should not do

I want to say this before I
Begin
You may disagree but I don't mean to offend
You are a Christian and I am too
Why do you disrespect me
And why do I disrespect you

If we are Christians that is something we should not do
Now I am going to pray for you
And you should pray for me too

There is so much going on in this world now
especially when it comes to politics and we
are all not going to agree politically.
Why do you disrespect me
And why do I disrespect you
If we are Christian this is something we should not do
Now I am going to pray for you and should pray for me too

This is what Christians do

Not everyone is going to agree with each other's life
style if we are Christian we should not call them names,
we should pray for them that things may change.

This is what Christians do

If we say we have never Sin
That's when the lies start
When will it end
Now we all know we should pray again

We as Christians should not talk about each other
We as Christians should pray for one another
And
Love all of our Sisters and Brothers!
No matter what Race, Creed or Color!

This is what Christians do

Brenda Miller Meyers
June 12, 2021

Thank our Lord Jesus Today

Lord I can't stop Crying
In this world now people are daily dying
All are not due to healthcare
It's due to guns everywhere

You have to be willing
To stop the killing
Stop the shooting
And all the looting
If you are trying to blame
Someone else you need to
Take a look at yourself

People are killing Mothers and Fathers, Children's even a
baby child if you are doing this you need to Pray out loud
Please stop these Killings

If you are trying to blame someone else
You need to take a look at yourself
Take Time to Pray
That you can take this Anger away

Things always get better when you Pray
Thank our Lord Jesus today

Brenda Miller Meyers
June 20, 2021

Lord Please Bring Back Love

People we need to Love Everyone
If we don't our Life is Done

Please bring back families and all the Fun
If we don't our Life is Done

You may not know me
I may not know you
We can still love each other
This I know is true
I am bringing back love
And I hope you do too

Please bring back families and all the Fun
If we don't our Life is Done

I don't have to be related to you
And you don't have to be related to me
We can still love each other

This I know is true
I am bringing back love
And I hope you do too

Brenda Miller Meyers
July 12, 2021

Lord we Blessed the things unseen

I know we all love material things
Let's start blessings the things unseen

We love the car we drive
Blessed being able to give someone a ride

We love living in our home that we own
Blessed being able to share your home
with someone that can't live alone

We love being able to afford the food we love to eat
Blessed someone by giving them a treat

If you have your finances under control
Blessed being able to give someone
a $1 that you don't know

Lord I know we all love material things
Let's start blessings the things unseen

Brenda Miller Meyers
July 22, 2021

Our Lord Jesus Christ always Shines

Those that knows our Lord Jesus Christ
Shines will always be Kind

If you see someone sitting on the streets ask
them if they need something to eat

Life always shines when you are kind

If you were blessed to never have experience hard times
Don't judge those that have
Just do something kind

Life always shines when you are kind

When you see someone on the corner with
a sign asking for a dollar or a dime
Don't judge them
Just do something kind

Life always shines when you are kind

When Life challenges brings you hard times don't give up
Just keep praying because our Lord Jesus
Christ always brings the shine

Our Lord Jesus Christ always Shines

Brenda Miller Meyers
July 29, 2021

God is Good all the time!

When you bring happiness to others-
Joy will always come to you!

God is Good all the time!

When you see someone you know looking sad, go
say something to them that will make them laugh!

God is Good all the time!

When you feel that you are going to have a bad day, go
to your mirror and smile, it will take your bad day away!

God is Good all the time!

When you Love yourself it's
always easier to Love someone else, always Love yourself!

God is Good all the time!

Brenda Miller Meyers
August 3, 2021

Lord we are all wanting
Peace and Safety

Let's pray for good news, that the
Gun fires, House fires and
Wild fires, ends soon!

We will pray everyday for Peace and Safety

Let's pray for good news, that the
earthquakes, floods, hurricanes, storms
And tornados, ends soon!

Last but not least people please stop
these car crashes some are
Leaving people in ashes!

We will pray everyday for Peace and Safety!

Brenda Miller Meyers
August 18, 2021

Take Time To Pray

I know we say that we don't have time
When we take time to Pray things will get better each
Day!

Say you looked at your checking account and noticed it's
Overdrawn!
You will probably scream Lord what did I do
Wrong!

When we take time to Pray things get better each
Day!

Say you get in your car and you noticed it's real low on gas
You check your wallet and scream Lord I am low on
Cash!

When we take time to Pray things get better each
Day!

We all experienced challenges in this
World, Men, Women, Boys and Girls

When we take time to Pray things get better each
Day!

Take Time to Pray!

Brenda Miller Meyers September 5, 3021

Have you Ever

Have you ever told someone a lie and because of your lie
it caused them to Cry!

Have you ever taken something that did not Belong
To you and when you were asked about it you lied
And said it was not You!

Have you ever called someone a name and when
Others heard you do it but you felt no Shame!

Have you ever asked a friend to help you with a
Bad situation and when they did it, you continue
To ask them again and again, when will it End!

If you have ever done any of these statements listed above
Please pray for forgiveness and pray to learn how to Love!

Have you Ever

Brenda Miller Meyers
September 11, 2021

Let's Pray Because We Can

Let's Pray for anyone that has recently
loss a family member or a friend

Why Because We Can
Amen!

Let's Pray for those that lost homes that they owned

Why Because We Can
Amen!

Let's Pray for those that have lost their jobs, and
can no longer pay their bills or eat a daily meal

Why Because We Can
Amen!

Let's Pray for the homeless that they will
be able to be placed into a home

Why Because We Can
Amen!

Let's Pray for all the statements listed above,
we want to Pray for Happiness and Love

Why Because We Can
Amen!

Brenda Miller Meyers
September 25th, 2021

God always works it out!

When you wake up in the morning feeling like you
did not get any Rest, Don't get Stressed, it's best
when you are not stressed now take a breath.

God always works it out!

Sometimes we are hit with unexpected challenges don't get
upset just stay balance, it will smooth out your challenges.

God always works it out!

Just a note: I always feel good when I smile, if you
see me smiling at you, when you smile back at
me you will feel good too, this I know is true.

God always works it out!

Smile ☺

Brenda Miller Meyers
October 4, 2021

Pray Your Hatred Stops Today

People please stop the Hate
I know you think about the bad things that you do, I
know you don't want bad things to happen to You!
Pray Your Hatred Stops Today

People please stop the Hate
When things go wrong in our life we want to blame
someone else, we never want to blame ourselves
and then we take the anger out on someone else!
Pray Your Hatred Stops Today

People Please stop the Hate
When you are doing physical harm to others,
setting Churches and Homes on fire, if doing
these things make you feel good, please pray that
it stops today and your anger and hatred goes
away so that your life can get better every day!

Please Note: The only Gain from causing Pain to others is
Shame, this we know is true and we are sure you do too!

Pray Your Hatred Stops Today

Brenda Miller Meyers
October 13, 2021

Please Forgive Us Lord

When the World Shakes
We all make Mistakes

Sometimes when we sit down
We don't want anyone around

When the phone Rings
We start to sing that silences the Ring

Sometimes we start conversations that some don't want
to have when we are asked to stop we start to laugh

Sometimes we say it's time to go to bed when we
look at our Clock, then when we wake up in the
morning we realize our door was not locked

Sometimes we pick up the phone and dialed
the wrong number, then we asked who are you
oops your not my sister or my brother

When the world Shakes
We all make Mistakes

Brenda Miller Meyers
October 25, 2021

Please Guide Me Lord

Should I stay in or should I go out
Should I scream or should I shout
Should I open or should I close my mouth
Please Guide Me Lord

When I went to visit a friend I knock on the door
she would not let me in should I scream or should I
shout should I open or should I close my mouth

When I went to the store to get an item that I
wanted the clerk said sorry we are out
Should I scream or should I shout should
I open or should I close my mouth

When I went to the post office to send a package
to a family member or a friend, the post office
clerk says that will be $40 to send.
Should I scream or should I shout should
I open or should I close my mouth

Please guide me Lord

Brenda Miller Meyers
November 7, 2021

Lord please give us
Strength to carry on!

When we think we can't go forward
we keep going backwards

When we think we can't solve the problems we
see I blame it on you and you blame it on me

When we look out the window and the sun don't
shine, do what you plan to do just take your time

When we are having a bad day we know what
to do read our Bible and take time to Pray.

Lord please give us strength to carry on!

Brenda Miller Meyers
November 22, 2021

What do we say? Pray Pray Pray

When you are having hard Times - Don't drink the Wine
Don't Spoke or do the Coke

We all know what happens to someone when
they go down that Road and it ain't no Joke

What do we say? Pray Pray Pray

We are not judging anyone that goes down that road,
we just want them to make better choices so that
they can get to be the person we used to know

What do we say? Pray Pray Pray

Please Note: We will always Love, Love, Love You!, we
just want to always be able to Hug, Hug, Hug You!

What do we say? Pray Pray Pray

Brenda Miller Meyers
December 11, 2021

Pray For those that are
Suicidal and use your Ear

Have you ever had a family member or a friend shared with you that they wanted to commit suicide, don't run from them or hide just listen and stand by their side I know this is something none of us want to hear your best support is your Ear, when you listen understanding is more clear

1. Don't judge them and call them weak, the best support is your Ear, when you listen your understandings is more clear
2. Please don't tell that it is something you don't want to hear the best support is your Ear, when you listen it is real clear

I know we tell them to call the suicide hotline sometimes it works and sometimes not all the time, how do I know because I have been there and what helped me was my friends Ear, when he listened his support was very clear and my suicide thoughts were no longer there, I thank God for my friends Ear

Brenda Miller Meyers
December 22, 2021

CPSIA information can be obtained
at www.ICGtesting.com
Printed in the USA
BVHW030506310322
632800BV00002B/172

9 781663 236418